Exploring Science
Invertebrates

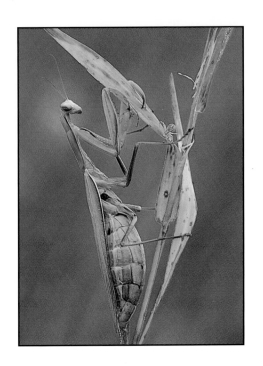

Invertebrates

Bradford Burnham

Thomson Learning

New York

A FRIEDMAN GROUP BOOK

First published in the
United States in 1995 by
Thomson Learning
New York, NY

Library of Congress Cataloging-in-Publication Data
Burnham, Brad.
    Invertebrates / Brad Burnham.
        p. cm. — (Exploring science)
    Includes bibliographical references and index.
    ISBN 1–56847–272–2
    1. Invertebrates—Juvenile literature. [1. Invertebrates.]
I. Title. II. Series: Exploring science (New York, N.Y.)
QL362.4.B87 1995
592—dc20

94-46317
CIP
AC

EXPLORING SCIENCE: INVERTEBRATES
was prepared and produced by
Michael Friedman Publishing Group, Inc.
15 West 26th Street
New York, New York 10010

Editor: Benjamin Boyington
Art Director/ Designer: Jeff Batzli
Photography Director: Christopher Bain
Photography Researchers: Christopher Bain and Susan Mettler
Illustrations: George Gilliland

Color separations by Benday Scancolour Co. Ltd.
Printed in China by Leefung-Asco Printed Ltd.

Dedication

To my mother, for her strength and wisdom

Acknowledgments

The author would like to thank many people
for their various contributions to this book:
Thomson Learning and the staff at the Michael Friedman
Publishing Group, especially Kelly Matthews, Ben
Boyington, and Jeff Batzli; the illustrators whose talent
gave dazzle to this book; and finally, Lisa Sita,
Karen Lund, Edward Dee, Ken Howell, Amy Van Allen,
and all my friends whose help and support
were as necessary to the completion of this book
as were pen and paper.

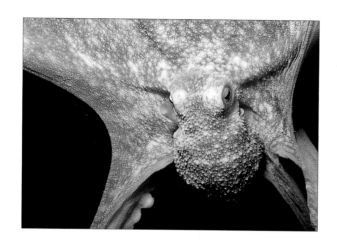

INTRODUCTION

WONDERS WITHOUT BACKBONES

INVERTEBRATES LIVE IN MANY DIFFERENT ENVIRONMENTS. THIS MARKET SQUID LIVES DEEP IN THE OCEAN.

INVERTEBRATES ALSO HAVE MANY DIFFERENT KINDS OF LIFESTYLES. THIS LEAF-CUTTER ANT IS A SOCIAL INVERTEBRATE; THIS MEANS THAT IT LIVES WITH MANY OTHER LEAF-CUTTER ANTS.

The world of **invertebrates** is a world of strange and wonderful creatures. More than one million kinds of invertebrates have been found throughout the world, and scientists believe that there may be millions more yet to be discovered. These animals, which make up more than 90 percent of the world's animal species, are very diverse in appearance and behavior. When it comes to size, for instance, many invertebrates are so small that they can be seen only with microscopes, while others, like giant squid, are so big that they can fight with sperm whales.

WHAT IS AN INVERTEBRATE?

Invertebrates are animals that do not have backbones; *in* means "without" and *vertebrate* means "backbone" in Latin. Animals with backbones, such as fish, reptiles, amphibians, birds, and mammals, are called **vertebrates**. The backbone in a vertebrate supports the animal's body. Inverte-

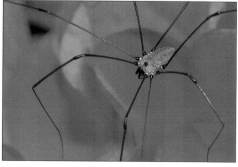

THE DADDY LONGLEGS IS A RELATIVE OF THE SPIDER.

Spineless Survey

To see how your friends and family feel about invertebrates, create a Spineless Survey. Begin by asking the following questions:

1. Do you know what an invertebrate is? (If they say yes, ask them to tell you. If they say no, explain it to them.)

2. Are you scared of any invertebrates? (If they say yes, ask what scares them—some don't like their looks, some are scared by sounds invertebrates make.)

3. Are there any invertebrates that you like? (If they say yes, ask which ones they like and why they like them.)

You can also ask any other questions you think up. But whatever you ask, once you have finished reading this book, make sure to go back to the people you surveyed and share with them some of what you have learned about invertebrates from this book: how quickly a bee must beat its wings to stay in the air, how there is a great diversity of shapes and sizes of invertebrates, and how important invertebrates can be in our daily lives.

brates, however, have other ways of supporting their bodies, such as hard, armorlike coverings, called **exoskeletons**, strong shells, and tough skin.

LIFESTYLES

The place where an animal lives and finds its food and shelter is called its **habitat**. A habitat may be as large as a forest or as small as the underside of a rock. People also have habitats—their homes, schools, places of work, grocery stores, and any other places they visit regularly.

Invertebrates live in many different habitats. In these habitats they have developed a wide range of **lifestyles,** or ways of fulfilling their basic requirements for survival (food and shelter, primarily). Examples of lifestyles and habitats include flightless flies that thrive on frozen mountaintops and tapeworms that live inside other animals.

THIS DRAGONFLY—WHICH IS PART OF THE LARGEST GROUP OF INVERTEBRATES (INSECTS)—IS COVERED WITH EARLY MORNING DEW.

They Live Where?

In California, petroleum fly larvae live in crude oil. They breathe through a tube that goes to the surface. They eat insects that get trapped in the oil.

In northern climates, Alaskan flies and Arctic beetles are able to survive temperatures as low as −76° F (−60°C).

THE GROUPS

Scientists group, or classify, animals according to what they have in common. In this process of classification, called **taxonomy**, the different groups are given different scientific names (usually taken from Greek or Latin, making the names difficult to pronounce and even harder to remember). Each type of plant and animal is classified into a series of groups and subgroups. The largest of the groups are the **kingdoms**, and the number of different kingdoms is continually being updated according

to new discoveries. Right now, the kingdom Plantae includes all plants, and the kingdom Animalia includes all vertebrate and invertebrate animals. Kingdoms are further divided into **phyla** (the plural form of the word **phylum**). Phyla are then divided into even smaller groups; the order of classification beneath phyla is **class, order, family, genus, species.** When scientists want to refer to an animal by its classification, they use its genus and species names; the familiar honeybee, for example, is called *Apis mellifera*, and

What Is a Species?

Each kind of animal or plant is a separate species, and each species is given a scientific name that is unique to it. Although many animals are similar in appearance, slight differences in lifestyle or body form are often enough to make them different species.

people are known as *Homo sapiens*.

There are about thirty-three invertebrate phyla in the kingdom Animalia. The smallest phylum contains

Everyday Classification

For a fun experiment in taxonomy, try classifying some of your belongings in the same way that scientists classify animals. Below are examples of the scientific classification for humans and monarch butterflies, along with a sample classification of a catcher's softball mitt.

The scientific names are difficult to pronounce and hard to remember, but some give you clues to the animal's nature and appear-

ance. For example, humans are classified in the kingdom Animalia, and within that kingdom they are classified as phylum Chordata (meaning that they have a certain kind of nerve cord called a **notochord**). Humans are in the class Mammalia, meaning that they are mammals (animals who give birth to live young).

If we skip to the last classification of humans, we see that the species name is *Homo sapiens*. To classify your belongings, make up fun classifications like the ones listed below (if you want, you can create your own classification groups).

Taxon	Human	Monarch Butterfly	Softball Mitt
Kingdom:	Animalia	Animalia	*Your things*
Phylum:	Chordata	Arthropoda	*Sports equipment*
Class:	Mammalia	Insecta	*Softball gear*
Order:	Primates	Lepidoptera	*Protection*
Family:	Hominidae	Danaidai	*Leather*
Genus:	Homo	Danaus	*Catcher*
Species:	sapiens	plexippus	*mitt*
Known as:	Homo sapiens	Danaus plexippus	*Catcher's mitt*

just a few species, but the largest, Arthropoda, contains close to a million. There is an amazing world of invertebrates out there just waiting to be discovered by anyone curious enough to look.

IN OUR LIVES

Invertebrates provide us with food, please us with their songs, intrigue us with their strangeness, and sometimes upset us with their behavior. Many invertebrates are pests that cause millions of dollars worth of damage each year, but many more help to recycle nutrients and maintain the health of many habitats. Regardless of the effect on their habitats, one thing is clear: invertebrates are important members of any environment.

Harmful Invertebrates

Invertebrates can do harm to crops and personal belongings, and can even be dangerous to people. A single housefly can carry up to six million disease-causing bacteria on its body hairs and legs. Mosquitoes, which are a kind of fly, are the most dangerous of the group. Female mosquitoes fly from one animal to another, sucking blood and often spreading diseases. Malaria is perhaps the most deadly of these diseases, killing close to one million people a year.

A MOSQUITO WITH AN ABDOMEN FULL OF BLOOD.

A COMMON HOUSEFLY.

Aphids, Colorado potato beetles, and other pests cause millions of dollars in damage each year to crops and stored food. Many pests, such as Japanese beetles, are unwanted guests from other countries. They arrive with food shipments and are able to thrive because their natural enemies, those animals who prey on them, do not exist in North America.

APHIDS CAUSE A LOT OF DAMAGE TO PLANTS BY PIERCING STEMS, LEAVES, AND BUDS TO DRINK THE PLANTS' VITAL FLUIDS.

Cockroach Woes

Cockroaches live in many homes across North America. They give off oils that smell bad, and they carry many germs on their bodies and feet. When they walk on your food and plates they leave their smelly droppings and germs behind. They are also very hard to kill—a cockroach that loses its head can still live for nine days.

Helpful Invertebrates

While many invertebrates seem to do nothing but harm people and their belongings, there are also many that are helpful to humans. Bees, butterflies, and moths help us indirectly by helping flowering plants to produce fruits and seeds. Spiders, dragonflies, ladybugs, and many species of wasp are predators of flies, aphids, caterpillars, beetles, and many other crop pests.

Many invertebrates are harvested as food and served around the world as delicacies. Crabs, lobsters, shrimp, clams, snails, squid, and insects are just a few of the invertebrates that wind up on our dinner plates.

Bee Renters

Because many farmers rely on bees to pollinate their plants, some beekeepers rent their bees to farmers of almonds, blueberries, apples, or cucumbers. The beekeepers load up a truck with their bees and travel from one farm to another.

ABOVE: BEES DRINKING NECTAR (THE RAW MATERIAL USED TO MAKE HONEY) FROM A SCOTCH THISTLE. BELOW: LADYBIRD BEETLES (OR LADYBUGS) ARE PERHAPS THE BEST KNOWN OF THE BEETLES. FARMERS AND GARDENERS LOVE THEM BECAUSE THEY EAT CROP PESTS SUCH AS APHIDS.

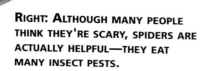

RIGHT: ALTHOUGH MANY PEOPLE THINK THEY'RE SCARY, SPIDERS ARE ACTUALLY HELPFUL—THEY EAT MANY INSECT PESTS.

Invertebrate Science

Scientists have discovered many interesting and useful things about invertebrates. These discoveries have given us many clues about nature and have helped improve medicine, agriculture, and other elements of human life.

Research is currently being conducted on a chemical called **chitin,** which acts as glue in insect wings and the exoskeletons of all arthropods (the name given to all creatures of the phylum Arthropoda).

Scientists believe that this chemical may have a great impact on the fields of medicine and agriculture.

Invertebrates are important members of nearly all the world's habitats. They influence our lives in ways that we are just beginning to understand. Scientists who study invertebrates, called **invertebrate zoologists**, have a never-ending job. Like these scientists, you will want to share with your friends and family your knowledge and curiosity about these wonders without backbones.

THESE SEVENTH-GRADERS ARE LEARNING HOW MONARCH BUTTERFLIES ARE TAGGED. BY TAGGING MONARCHS, SCIENTISTS HOPE TO LEARN MORE ABOUT THEIR BEHAVIOR.

Spineless Journal

Another fun (and easy) thing to do is to create a journal to record the invertebrates you see.

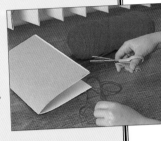

1. Find some blank paper— white or recycled—and a sheet of construction paper. Take a few sheets of the blank paper (you can always add more later) and fold them in half; use the piece of construction paper as the cover for this journal (put it at the bottom of the blank paper and fold the stack up toward you).

2. Ask an adult to help you, and make at least two holes along the fold. Weave a piece of yarn or string through the holes and tie the ends together where they meet in the back.

3. Write your name on the cover. You now have a journal you can write and draw in.

Whenever you see an invertebrate, draw it as best you can and write down what color it was, and where and when you found it.

CHAPTER ONE

CREEPY-CRAWLIES: INSECTS AND SPIDERS

Sizing Them Up

Insects come in all sizes. The smallest known insects are hairy-winged beetles that live in the tropics and are 1/100 inch (0.25 millimeters) long. The longest known insects are stick insects (above) that live in the tropics and grow to be more than a foot (0.3 meters) long.

INSECTS

Insects are the most diverse of all the invertebrates: there are more kinds of insects than there are all other invertebrates com-

bined. Scientists who study insects, called **entomologists**, are continually finding new species of insects, and they believe that there may be thousands, maybe even millions, yet to be discovered. Insects are the only invertebrates that can fly. Because of this, they are able to live almost anywhere on Earth. About the only place insects do not live is in the ocean, but they do live in most land and freshwater environments.

ENTOMOLOGISTS STUDY THE BIOL-
OGY, BEHAVIOR, AND ECOLOGY OF
INSECTS. SOME CONDUCT THEIR
STUDIES IN LABORATORIES WHILE
OTHERS TRAVEL TO FARAWAY
PLACES TO OBSERVE INSECTS IN
THEIR NATURAL HABITATS.

Body

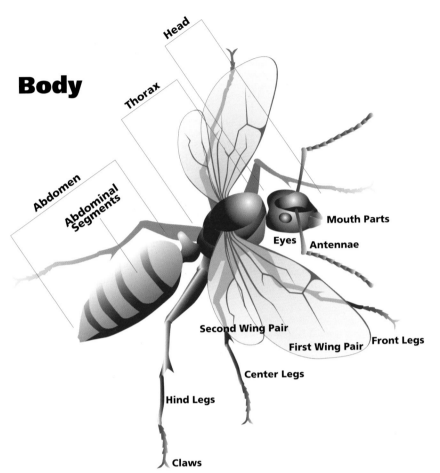

Head

Thorax

Abdomen

Abdominal Segments

Mouth Parts

Eyes

Antennae

Second Wing Pair

First Wing Pair

Front Legs

Center Legs

Hind Legs

Claws

Body of Armor

Insects' bodies are covered by a thick skin, called an **exoskeleton**, that is covered with a protective waxy coating to prevent water loss. This strong protective coating enables insects to survive in many different environments.

An insect's body has three main parts: the **head**, the **thorax** (the central section), and the **abdomen**. Their heads have feelers, called **antennae**, that are sensitive to touch and smell, and mouth parts that come in many different sizes and

shapes, depending on what the insect eats. Some mouths are large and wide; others are long and thin. Most adult insects have one or two pairs of wings attached at the thorax. All insects have six legs that also attach to the body at the thorax. The legs are segmented and have a pair of claws at each end. These claws make it possible for insects to get a firm grip on plants, animals, or the walls of your house.

Inside the abdomen are the reproductive organs and most of the digestive system. For some insects, the abdomen is also where the stinger or some other defense mechanism is located.

IN ADDITION TO HAVING A HARD EXOSKELETON, BUTTERFLIES AND MOTHS HAVE SCALES ON THEIR BODIES AND WINGS. THE SCALES, WHICH ARE VERY TINY, COME IN MANY COLORS.

MOST INSECTS HAVE BOTH COMPOUND AND SIMPLE EYES. THE COMPOUND EYES ARE USUALLY LARGE AND COVER MOST OF THE HEAD. THE SIMPLE EYES ARE POSITIONED IN BETWEEN THE COMPOUND EYES.

Sensing the World

Insects' sensory organs are very different from those of people. Most adult insects have two kinds of eyes: large **compound eyes** and small **simple eyes**. Compound eyes are made up of hundreds of small lenses, each with its own light-sensitive cells. A housefly may have up to four thousand lenses in each compound eye, and a dragonfly

Observation Kit

With the help of an adult, make an Observation Kit.

1. Find a plastic container, such as a plastic peanut butter jar, and clean it out.

2. Ask an adult to make a few very small holes in the lid. These holes will give the insect fresh air to breathe. Most invertebrates that you can find near your house are harmless and can easily be captured, but be careful—some are harmful to people.

3. With the help of an adult, go out and collect an invertebrate. Use the jar to scoop it up; if possible, you should also take home the object you found the invertebrate on.

4. At home, while the invertebrate is in the jar, look closely at it. Can you draw it in your Spineless Journal? What color is it? How many legs does it have? Is it a fast crawler? Does it have wings?

Collecting invertebrates can be very rewarding. Caterpillars, beetles, grasshoppers, fireflies, ants, and pond insects are all easy to catch and interesting to observe.

When you use your Observation Kit to collect invertebrates, always note where you found a certain creature so you can return it to its proper habitat later.

You can also observe invertebrates in the wild (in their natural habitats). With adult supervision, these creatures may be seen year-round. Before hunting for invertebrates, ask someone who works with wildlife in your area about any dangerous or endangered animals you should avoid. In the northern parts of North America, insects are most active in the mid-summer and early autumn months. While observing an invertebrate in its natural habitat, you may learn what it eats, where it hides, and how it interacts with other animals.

may have up to twenty-five thousand! You would expect that with all these lenses insects would have good eyesight, but this is not the case. Scientists have found that people can see images a hundred times more sharply than honeybees can.

Insects smell and feel the world around them with their antennae. Some insects have very sensitive antennae and are able to smell some scents from miles away. The shape and size of the antennae depend on where and how the insect lives. An insect that lives in the ground, such as a mole cricket, has short, thick antennae that are not easily damaged. But an insect that flies a lot, such as a cockchafer beetle, has long, fragile antennae to sense changes in the wind. Antennae come in so many different shapes and sizes that they can often be used to identify the insect.

Their Ear Is Where?

Honeybees, mosquitoes, and flies hear with their antennae, but some insects actually have earlike structures. Crickets have an "ear" on each of their front legs, locusts have a small, earlike membrane on their bodies at the beginning of their rear legs, and cicadas have large membranes on the undersides of their bodies that act like ears.

LIKE MOST MOTHS, THIS POLYPHEMUS MOTH HAS LARGE FEATHERY ANTENNAE, WHICH ARE USED TO DETECT SMELLS AND MAY ALSO HELP TO DETECT SOUND.

Smile!

There are many different kinds of insect mouths, but chewing or sucking mouth parts are the most common. Large jaws are good for cutting or crushing hard food, and long, tubelike mouths are good for sipping liquids. Houseflies have spongelike mouth parts that they use to soak up liquids, fleas have needlelike mouth parts that they use to pierce skin and drink blood, and ant lion larvae have large, sharp jaws that they use to catch and kill ants.

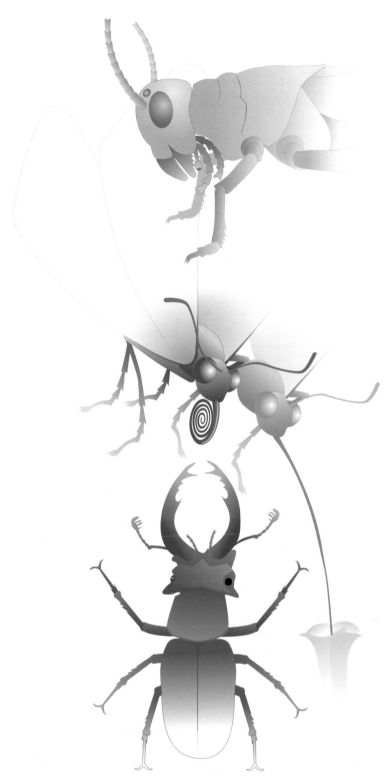

INSECT MOUTH PARTS COME IN A VARIETY OF SHAPES AND SIZES. THE GRASSHOPPER (TOP) AND THE MALE STAG BEETLE (BOTTOM) HAVE MOUTH PARTS CALLED **MANDIBLES**, WHICH ARE USED TO BITE AND CHEW. THE BUTTERFLY (MIDDLE), HOWEVER, HAS A LONG, SUCKING MOUTH PART CALLED A **PROBOSCIS**, WHICH IT UNROLLS AND USES TO SUCK NECTAR FROM FLOWERING PLANTS.

Is It a Bug?

Many people call anything that crawls a "bug," but in fact this word refers to a group of insects that have tubelike mouth parts designed for piercing or sucking. This group includes assassin bugs, bedbugs, stink bugs, and aquatic bugs such as giant water bugs like the one above.

Out-of-Body Experience

Houseflies start digesting their meals before they even eat them. They do this by spitting digestive juices onto their food. These juices turn the meal into liquids that their spongelike mouths can absorb. Unfortunately, they often spread diseases as they drool on their food.

ALTHOUGH THE LARGE JAWS, ALSO CALLED "ANTLERS," OF THIS MALE STAG BEETLE GIVE IT A FIERCE APPEARANCE, THIS INSECT DOES NOT HAVE A STRONG BITE.

A BUTTERFLY HAS A LONG, THIN MOUTH PART CALLED A PROBOSCIS (BELOW ANTENNAE, EXTENDING FROM MOUTH TO FLOWER), WHICH IT USES TO REACH THE NECTAR INSIDE FLOWERS. WHEN THE BUTTERFLY IS IN FLIGHT, THE PROBOSCIS ROLLS UP INTO A TIGHT COIL.

AN INSECT'S MOUTH IS SHAPED AND SIZED ACCORDING TO WHAT IT EATS. THIS LUBBER GRASSHOPPER EATS TOUGH LEAVES, SO IT HAS VERY STRONG JAWS.

Pliers and Drills

Some beetles' jaws, or **mandibles**, act as pliers, and are so strong that the beetle can bite through copper and lead! Weevils drill and pry into food with tiny mouths at the ends of their long beaks, or **rostrums**, causing tremendous damage each year to stored food.

THE HALLOWEEN DRAGONFLY IS ABLE TO MAKE QUICK MOVEMENTS THROUGH THE AIR.

Flying Invertebrates

Most adult insects can fly. Flying has many advantages. It allows insects to escape predators faster and to cover more ground as they search for food or a mate. Insect wings are thin, lightweight folds of their exoskeleton. They are fragile and great care must be taken to keep them safe. Beetles use their front pair of wings to protect the rear pair, which are used for flying. The second pair unfolds from underneath the first pair and spreads out when the beetle wants to fly.

SOME INSECTS, LIKE THESE YELLOW JACKETS, SEEM TO HAVE ONLY ONE PAIR OF WINGS. IN FACT, THEY HAVE A SECOND PAIR THAT ARE VERY HARD TO SEE.

INSECT WINGS COME IN A WIDE RANGE OF FORMS. THE BUTTERFLY (LEFT) HAS BROAD, SAIL-LIKE WINGS FOR FLUTTERING IN THE BREEZE; THE BEETLE (MIDDLE) HAS HARD FRONT WINGS TO PROTECT ITS DELICATE HIND WINGS, WHICH ARE USED FOR FLYING; AND THE DRAGONFLY (RIGHT) HAS LONG, LIGHT WINGS, WHICH ENABLE IT TO DART BACK AND FORTH RAPIDLY THROUGH THE AIR.

ALTHOUGH IT SEEMS UNLIKELY, MANY STRANGE-LOOKING INSECTS, LIKE THIS STAG BEETLE WITH ITS LARGE JAWS, ARE ACTUALLY ABLE TO FLY.

Many insects are able to fly quite fast. Hummingbird moths and horseflies have been recorded at speeds of up to 33 miles per hour (53 kilometers per hour). Some insects need to beat their wings rapidly to stay in the air—honeybees and houseflies beat their wings 190 times each second, and some gnats need to beat theirs a thousand times per second to stay aloft. Butterflies and grasshoppers, however, are able to beat their wings slowly and still stay in the air.

LEFT: BUTTERFLIES, LIKE THIS BLACK SWALLOWTAIL, CANNOT FOLD THEIR WINGS LIKE OTHER INSECTS, SO WHEN THEY LAND THEY HOLD THEIR WINGS TOGETHER AND UPRIGHT. BELOW: CLOSE-UP OF A BLACK SWALLOWTAIL'S WING.

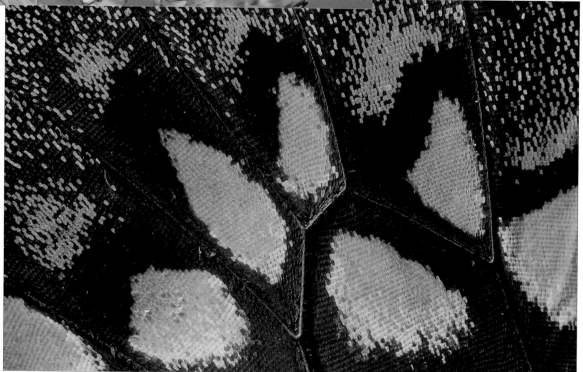

Relatives of Insects

With three times more species than all other animal phyla combined, Arthropoda is the largest phylum in the kingdom Animalia. Insects, centipedes, crabs, scorpions, lobsters, and spiders are members of the phylum Arthropoda. All arthropods have hard exoskeletons and jointed legs; only insects have six legs and wings.

WHILE INSECTS HAVE SIX LEGS, CENTIPEDES SEEM TO HAVE A HUNDRED. IN FACT, THEY ARE NAMED FOR THEIR MANY LEGS—IN LATIN, *CENTI* MEANS "ONE HUNDRED" AND *PEDE* MEANS "FOOT."

SPIDERS ARE NOT INSECTS, BUT ARE IN A CLASS OF INVERTEBRATES CALLED ARACHNIDA. OTHER MEMBERS OF THIS CLASS INCLUDE SCORPIONS, TICKS, AND MITES.

SPIDERS

The thirty-four thousand or more species of spiders in the world are predators of insects, other small invertebrates, and even small vertebrate animals. Some spiders catch their prey with webs, while others use quick jumps. The complex webs that many spiders make can be found in lawns, fields, forests, and even people's homes. Spiders are welcome in many homes because they eat a variety of insect pests.

The Body

Spiders are members of the phylum Arthropoda, and within this phylum they are in a group, or class, of animals called Arachnida. Like insects, spiders have exoskeletons and jointed legs. Unlike insects, though, spiders have eight eyes (usually), eight legs, only two body segments, and glands that produce silk.

The bodies of spiders are divided into two segments: an abdomen and a **cephalothorax**. The abdomen, which is often very large, contains many of the spider's organs, such as the silk glands and the reproductive organs. The cephalothorax is a combination of the head and the midsection of the body. The legs are situated in the middle of the cephalothorax, and the pair of fangs, the eyes, and the pair of sensory feelers, called **palps**, are located at the front.

Spiders have strong and fast-acting poisons that are used to paralyze or kill their prey. Most spiders' poisons can harm only small animals, but a few kinds of spiders have poisons that can hurt (or even kill) large animals. A bite from some North American spiders can be harmful to humans. Tarantulas can make you sick, but brown recluses and black widows are *very* dangerous—a bite from one of these spiders will make you very ill.

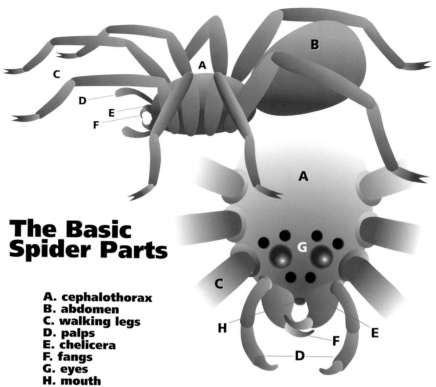

The Basic Spider Parts

A. cephalothorax
B. abdomen
C. walking legs
D. palps
E. chelicera
F. fangs
G. eyes
H. mouth

BLACK WIDOWS ARE BEAUTIFUL, BUT HUMANS SHOULD KEEP THEIR DISTANCE—THESE SPIDERS HAVE STRONG VENOM.

IF YOU WERE ABLE TO GET CLOSE ENOUGH, YOU COULD SEE A SPIDER'S FANGS AND EYES.

Stylish Webs

There are a variety of web types, but most web-building spiders build **orb webs**. To build an orb web, a spider first makes the framework between two objects, then finishes by spiraling out from the center.

Some spiders build **funnel webs**. They then hide in the narrow mouth of the funnel and wait for insects to get trapped. When an insect does get tangled in the funnel web, the spider runs out and pulls it back into the mouth of the web.

Bolas spiders of the southeastern United States do not build webs at all. They attach a drop of sticky fluid to a dangled silk thread and try to lasso passing insects.

Spinning Silk

While spider silk is best known for its uses in webs, most spiders have six or seven different kinds of silk that they use for different purposes. Some kinds are used only for creating webs, others are used for wrapping prey, and some have strong smells and are used for attracting mates.

Female spiders use their silk to protect eggs and young by spinning it into spheres, flattened disks, or even large nurseries. Newly hatched baby spiders, called **spiderlings**, use silk to "balloon" away to new and faraway hunting grounds. To do this, young spiders go to the end of a branch or leaf,

TOP RIGHT: FEMALE SPIDER WITH EGG SAC. THE EGGS INSIDE ARE PROTECTED BY THE MANY STRANDS OF WEB MAKING UP THE CASE. RIGHT: THESE SPIDERLINGS ARE USING THEIR SILK TO GO "BALLOONING." WHEN A BREEZE CATCHES THE STRANDS OF SILK, THE SPIDERLINGS ARE LIFTED INTO THE AIR AND CARRIED AWAY.

spin long threads of silk, and wait for a gust of wind. When the wind catches their silk threads, it whisks them up and away into the air. They may get blown many miles before landing and finding a new home. Young spiders have been seen "ballooning" at heights of 14,000 feet (4,267 meters) and more than two hundred miles (320 kilometers) out to sea.

Some web-making spiders build webs that seem to be messy bunches of tangled strands, while others create webs that seem to have very specific designs. No matter how well constructed the webs are, though, they are usually torn down and eaten at the end of the night.

A spider "hunts" by waiting in the middle or off to one side of its web. When an animal is caught in a web, its struggles send vibrations down the strands of the web to the spider. When the spider senses these vibrations, it runs out to the trapped animal, wraps it in silk, and kills (or paralyzes) it with the

Silky Surprise

Trapdoor spiders spin their silk into trapdoors that they place on top of their burrows. A trapdoor spider is always ready to offer an invitation of welcome to any small passersby. It jumps out of its burrow, grabs the insect with its strong front legs, and pulls it inside. But instead of serving the insect a meal, the spider serves the insect as the meal.

A BURROWING WOLF SPIDER AWAITS ITS PREY.

Web Wetting

Spiderwebs are easy to see in the early morning because the morning dew clings to their strands. If you want to observe some webs, you can create your own morning dew any time of day with a spray bottle full of water.

Search for webs inside your house and outside in your backyard, neighborhood, or park.

When you locate a web, first look for the spider—just to be safe—and make sure it is a species that cannot cause you harm. Then set the spray bottle on fine spray and lightly spray the web.

Is the web an orb web? Are there any insects caught in the web? Visit the same location on another day to see if the spider is still making webs and hunting there.

poison in its fangs. When a spider bites its prey, it injects not only poison but chemicals that begin to turn the victim's insides to liquid that the spider can easily eat.

Feel the Vibrations

Web-building spiders are very good at detecting vibrations along the strands of their webs. So when a male spider approaches a female's web he taps a message of announcement so that the larger female won't run out and eat him.

WEB-BUILDING SPIDERS "HUNT" BY WAITING PATIENTLY ON THEIR WEBS UNTIL THEY FEEL THE VIBRATIONS OF A TRAPPED VICTIM ON THE WEB'S SILK, THEN RUNNING QUICKLY OUT TO THE PREY AND INJECTING IT WITH POISON. RIGHT: A GOLDEN ORB SPIDER, A NATIVE OF SOUTH AMERICA.

LEFT: SOME ARACHNIDS, LIKE THIS CRAB SPIDER, HAVE CAMOUFLAGE THAT ALLOWS THEM TO HUNT BY BLENDING INTO THE BACKGROUND.

Jumping Spiders

There are about three hundred species of **cursorial**, or running and jumping, spiders in North America. They hunt during the day and settle down in crevices or silk cocoons at night. Because cursorial spiders have two large eyes among their six smaller eyes, they have very good eyesight. Their legs are usually heavier and stronger than those of web-building spiders, and they are able to jump as high as seven or eight inches (18 or 20 centimeters). They do not use their silk to spin webs, but to serve as safety lines, called **draglines**. Jumping spiders attach these draglines to leaves or branches as they hunt, and use the lines to catch themselves if they miss a target and fall.

JUMPING SPIDERS, WHICH DO NOT SPIN WEBS, HUNT BY RUNNING AFTER THEIR PREY (OR LYING IN WAIT FOR THEM) AND POUNCING UPON THEM. JUMPING SPIDERS ARE VERY FAST, AS IS SHOWN BY THEIR ABILITY TO CATCH RESTING FLIES BEFORE THEY CAN FLY AWAY.

Slight of Eye

Jumping spiders have very good eyesight and can see much better than web-building spiders. Some kinds of jumping spiders are even able to change the color of their eyes! There are probably many people who would like to be able to do that.

Relatives of Spiders

Scorpions, daddy longlegs, mites, and ticks are also arachnids (members of the class Arachnida). Their bodies are very similar to those of spiders.

There are about twenty to thirty species of scorpions in North America. Most of them live in warm, dry environments, but one species lives as far north as Canada. Scorpions have poison stingers attached to the rear of their tail-like abdomens, but they sting mostly in self-defense; they prefer to use their pincers to catch and kill prey. The venom in their stingers can easily kill small animals, and some North American scor- pions have venom that is strong enough to harm people. The world's most dangerous scorpions live in Mexico, South America, and North Africa.

A MAGNIFIED VIEW OF THE COMMON TICK (MANY TIMES ITS ACTUAL SIZE).

There are about twenty thousand species of mites in the world, and probably many more yet to be discov- ered. Mites live in fresh water, in salt water, and on

USING THE STINGER ON ITS TAIL-LIKE ABDOMEN, THIS SCULP- TURED SCORPION INJECTS A VENOM THAT IS TOXIC ENOUGH TO KILL INSECTS AND SMALL ANIMALS.

land. Most are parasites of plants or animals, and some transmit diseases. Some live only in bird feathers, others live under bat wings, and some even live in monkey lungs. Ticks are the largest kind of mites. They suck the blood of mammals, birds, and reptiles. A tick attaches itself to an animal and waits for another ani- mal to pass by.

CHAPTER TWO

SLIP SLIDIN' AWAY: SNAILS, SLUGS, AND WORMS

SNAILS ARE INVERTEBRATES WITH PROTECTIVE SHELLS THAT COME IN MANY DIFFERENT SHAPES AND SIZES. THIS GREEN SNAIL HAS A SMOOTH, PERFECTLY SPIRALED SHELL.

Taking Care of Snails or Slugs

If you decide you would like to keep a couple of snails or slugs as pets, you will find that they are very easy to take care of. All these invertebrates need is a clean, moist environment.

1. Line a clean jar or aquarium with moist paper towels. (White paper towels are best, because they have fewer chemical dyes.)

2. To prevent the snail or slug from escaping, cover the jar or aquarium with wire mesh or another material that will allow air in.

3. The snails or slugs may eat the paper towel, but you should also occasionally feed them pieces of lettuce or some other soft vegetable. Keep the towels moist. If the snail tucks itself into its shell, this may mean that there is not enough moisture in the container.

4. To keep the snails or slugs happy and healthy, clean the container about once a week.

SNAILS AND SLUGS

Snails and slugs are members of the phylum Mollusca, which is a phylum of "soft-bodied" animals. Snails and slugs can be found living in fresh water, salt water, and many land habitats. They are fun to observe as they leave trails of mucus over leaves, the ground, and even your hand if you pick them up.

The Shell Game

Snails' soft bodies are protected from injury by hard shells and a covering of thick mucus. A snail's shell is a mobile home that protects the snail from drying out and serves as a defense against predators. The shell grows as the snail grows. Tissue near the shell's opening, called the **mantle**, causes the shell to form interesting and often beautiful spiral shapes as it grows. Snail shells come in many different shapes and sizes. Some are long and thin; others are short and wide.

When a snail is threatened, it pulls its entire body into its shell and covers the opening with a hard, shell-like disk called an **operculum**. A snail will also tuck itself into its shell when its habitat becomes dry and water is unavailable.

Pearly Problem

A pearl forms when a piece of sand or dirt gets stuck near the mantle of an oyster or a clam, both of which are relatives of snails. Shell material called **mother-of-pearl** is slowly layered over the piece of dirt to protect the body's soft parts from injury. Over a period of many years, a pearl is formed. Most pearls are not as round and perfect as the ones used in jewelry.

The Basic Snail Parts

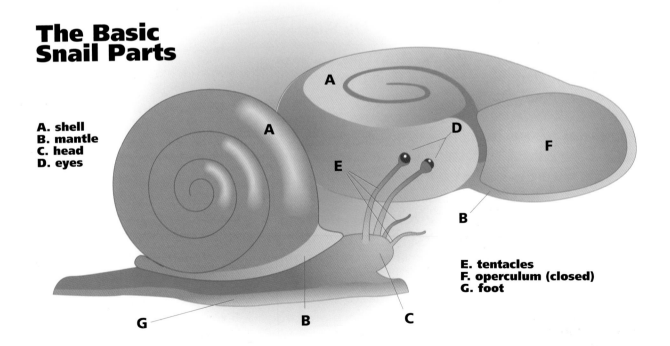

A. shell
B. mantle
C. head
D. eyes

E. tentacles
F. operculum (closed)
G. foot

SLUGS, WHICH ARE COMMON GAR-
DEN PESTS, ARE SIMILAR TO SNAILS
EXCEPT THAT THEIR SHELLS ARE
INTERNAL AND CANNOT BE SEEN.

Footsies

All mollusks have feet that are specialized for their lifestyles. Snails and slugs are in the class Gastropoda (from the Latin *gastro*, meaning "stomach," and *pod*, meaning "foot"). Squid and octopuses are in the class Cephalopoda, meaning "head foot," because their foot is divided up into tentacles and is directly attached to their head. Clams and oysters are in the class Bivalve, which used to be called Pelecypoda, or "hatchet foot," because their foot can be spread out into the shape of a hatchet's blade as it anchors them in the

Head First

Snails and slugs (which are basically snails without shells) sense the world around them using **tentacles**, which are flexible and sensitive to smell and touch. They reach out with their four tentacles and gently touch objects, quickly pulling back if the object is unfamiliar or dangerous. They may also have two simple eyes located at the ends of their tentacles. Simple eyes are able to sense changes in light intensity, but are unable to form clear images.

In their mouths, snails and slugs have tonguelike structures called **radulas**. These radulas have hundreds of tiny teeth on them. The teeth, which are lined up in rows, are used to rip food into small, easy-to-swallow pieces. Not all snails eat the same food. Some are **herbivores** (they eat only plants), while others are **scavengers** (they eat decaying plants and animals). Some are even cannibals—they eat other snails and slugs!

Gliding On Slime

Snails and slugs glide on a thin layer of mucus that covers everything they crawl across. The mucus protects the body and the hundreds of hairlike **cilia** on the bottom of the snail's single foot. The foot is this invertebrate's means of locomotion. The cilia and the large muscles in the foot work together to move the animal forward. The foot, which is quite large, also contains the snail's stomach. For this reason, snails and slugs are classified as **gastropods,** which means "stomach foot."

Relatives of Snails and Slugs

Oysters, clams, squid, and octopuses are also soft-bodied animals in the phylum Mollusca. Oysters, clams, and mussels filter organic matter (small pieces of plants and animals) out of the water. To feed, they open their two shells just enough to suck in water. When threatened,

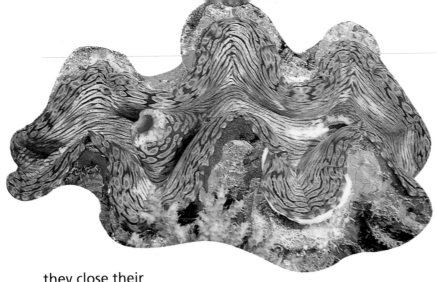

LEFT: **WHILE MOST INVERTEBRATES ARE SMALL, SOME ARE VERY LARGE. GIANT CLAMS CAN GROW TO BE MANY FEET TALL AND WIDE, AND RESEARCHERS HAVE DOCUMENTED GIANT SQUID THAT WERE CLOSE TO SIXTY FEET (18 METERS) LONG.**

they close their shells tightly for protection. Squid and octopuses are very different from snails and slugs in both behavior and appearance. They are fast-swimming predators that have strong tentacles that they use to catch their prey. Some even have poisons. The phylum Mollusca contains many interesting soft-bodied animals that live deep in the ocean. Snails and slugs, though, can be found in many land habitats, and are easy to find and observe.

BELOW: **THERE ARE MANY BEAUTIFUL INVERTEBRATES IN THE WORLD'S OCEANS. SEA SLUGS, OR NUDIBRANCHS, HAVE VERY COLORFUL AND STRANGE-LOOKING BODIES.**

Deadly Mollusk

The world's most potent venom comes from a mollusk that lives in Australia. The 6-inch (15-centimeter) blue-ringed octopus, shown at right, has a poison called **tetrodotoxin** that can kill a person in just a few minutes.

WORMS

In nature there are many **vermiform**, or wormlike, animals whose bodies are longer than they are wide. The phylum Annelida contains many of these animals, such as earthworms, clam worms, and leeches.

EARTHWORMS, KNOWN BY FISHERMEN EVERYWHERE AS NIGHT CRAWLERS, LIVE IN MOIST SOIL.

Earthworms

Earthworms have bodies that are **segmented**, or divided into many parts. Because of this, they appear to be made of many small rings. The rings, or segments, change shape as the earthworm moves along the ground. As a segment lengthens, it moves forward and is anchored to the ground with short, hairlike structures called **satae**. The segment then shortens, pulling the rest of the body forward with it.

Earthworms sense the world around them with cells that are located along the length of their bodies. These cells are sensitive to touch, smell, and light. The light-sensitive cells can detect the presence of direct sunlight, which is important because direct sunlight is dangerous for earthworms. They breathe through their moist skin, and if they stay in direct sunlight for too long their skin dries out and they suffocate.

Earthworms eat small pieces of food that they filter out of the soil as they tunnel through it. They also feed by coming out of their burrows at night to collect leaves and decaying matter, which they then take back underground. Their burrows criss-cross through gardens, lawns, and forests. Their waste, called **castings**, can be found around burrow openings. Earthworms are helpful invertebrates. As they tunnel, air is mixed into the soil. This helps plants grow, and because of this gardeners are always happy to see these invertebrates.

Taking Care of Earthworms

Earthworms can be kept in much the same way as snails or slugs. Put loose, moist soil (which you should take from the same place you get your worms) in a glass or plastic container. Do not use sand or clay—they are not good for earthworms because they are too hard and do not stay moist. Keep the container out of direct sunlight and keep the soil moist by misting it, or spraying it with water, once in a while. Feed the earthworms every week or two by sprinkling bread crumbs, cornmeal, or leaves on top of the soil. Clean out uneaten food before it starts to rot. For a closer look at your earthworms, just place one on a moist cloth or a damp paper towel.

After the Rain

During a rainstorm, earthworms may get flooded out of their tunnels. Because they breathe through their skin, they will drown in a flooded burrow. When the clouds clear and the sun shines, many worms get stranded on sidewalks and streets. If they do not return quickly to their burrows, they will dry up and die in the hot sun.

Clam Worms

Clam worms live in the sand and mud along shorelines. They are predators of clams, worms, snails, and other small invertebrates. Unlike earthworms, clam worms have eyes and tentacles to aid them in finding food. They have footlike structures, called **parapodia**, that move back and forth, pushing them through sand. The parapodia are also used for breathing—the skin on them is very thin and air passes in and out of them quite easily. Clam worms' jaws are usually tucked away in their mouths, but are pushed out for defense and for feeding. Their large, sharp jaws can give painful bites to predators, prey, and even people (if they are not careful).

Other Vermiform Animals

Flukes and leeches are **parasites**, meaning that they live and feed off many animals. Some flukes have life cycles that involve living in more than one animal. Sheep liver flukes are parasites of both sheep and snails, and they spend part of their lives living in each of these animals.

Leeches are parasites of animals that live in water, and may even attach themselves to swimming people. Like ticks, they feed by attaching themselves to a host and sucking its blood. When they are full, they fall off to digest the meal.

Wormlike animals thrive in many habitats, including gardens, lawns, ponds, and even inside other animals. Earthworms and clam worms can be just as interesting as the other vermiform creatures, once you have started to discover their unique lifestyles.

CLAM WORMS CAN BE FOUND ON MANY BEACHES AND MUD FLATS DURING LOW TIDE.

Traveling Parasites

The life cycle of a sheep liver fluke is complex. It hatches from an egg laid in fresh water. It then invades a snail's body and grows until it is ready to live in a sheep. To find a sheep, it leaves the snail's body, swims through the water, and attaches itself to plants along the shore. It is then eaten by a sheep grazing along the shore. Once inside the sheep's body, the fluke continues to grow, and eventually lays eggs. The eggs pass out of the sheep and into fresh water, where the cycle begins again.

Are Two Halves Better Than One?

Many vermiform animals can survive being cut in half. For instance, if a **planaria** (a certain kind of worm) is cut in half, each half will usually survive and will grow into a new worm.

CHAPTER THREE

THE FAMILY

APHIDS REPRODUCE VERY RAPIDLY. BY QUICKLY PRODUCING LOTS OF OFF-SPRING, THE CHANCES THAT SOME APHIDS WILL LIVE TO THE AGE OF REPRODUCTION TO CONTINUE THE SPECIES ARE GREATLY INCREASED.

So Little Time

Because white mayflies live for only an hour and a half as adults, they gather in large mating swarms. When they die they cover the streets with a blanket of dead bodies. Sometimes there are so many bodies that snowplows are needed to clear them away.

GROWTH AND REPRODUCTION

Because they live in so many different habitats and have such different lifestyles, invertebrates reproduce in many different ways. Finding a mate, producing eggs, and helping the next generation begin can be very difficult for small invertebrates. Many invertebrates spend a great deal of time and energy raising young, while others abandon their young very early, leaving them to chance and to predators.

Finding The Perfect Mate

The first step in reproduction is for a male and female to find each other. Invertebrates have very effective ways of using sound, smell, and even light to attract mates. The familiar chirping sound made by male crickets is the result of them rubbing their wings together. This sound attracts all females within hearing range. Male mole crickets also have a special mating call. They can increase the volume of their call, enabling them to reach many more females, by digging a Y-shaped tunnel near the surface of the ground. Male cicadas need no help—their call can be heard by females more than four hundred yards (366 meters) away.

Female silkworm moths, like many other insects, use chemicals called **phero-mones** to attract mates. Adult male silkworm moths have such sensitive antennae that they can smell the female's scent from up to seven miles (11 kilometers) away!

Noisy Bugs

Every seventeen years in the eastern United States, periodical cicadas emerge from the ground as adults and spend the last two weeks of their lives trying to find a mate. The shrill calls that the males make are very loud, and can be heard not only by female cicadas but by many surprised people as well.

Fireflies and glowworms produce flashing lights to attract mates. Their **luminescence**, sometimes called **cold light**, produces little or no heat. This light is being studied by scientists for possible uses by people.

ABOVE: **CRICKETS ARE FAMOUS FOR THEIR NIGHTTIME CHIRPING. THEY MAKE THIS SOUND, WHICH IS ACTUALLY THEIR MATING CALL, BY RUBBING THEIR FOREWINGS TOGETHER. BELOW: FIREFLIES ARE MISNAMED; THEY ARE ACTUALLY SOFT-BODIED BEETLES. ADULT FIREFLIES ATTRACT MATES WITH THE LIGHT THEY GENERATE IN THEIR ABDOMENS.**

SOME FEMALE APHIDS ARE BORN WITH THE ABILITY TO GIVE BIRTH WITHOUT MATING WITH A MALE APHID.

Where's the Romance?

Not all invertebrates need to mate with a member of the opposite sex in order to reproduce. Some female aphids can produce young female aphids without the male's sperm. This kind of reproduction is called **parthenogenesis**. Most invertebrates, however, do need to have eggs and sperm mix. There does not always have to be one male and one female, though. Earthworms and snails are **hermaphrodites**, meaning that each individual is both male and female. When two hermaphrodites meet they each give the other sperm to mix with eggs.

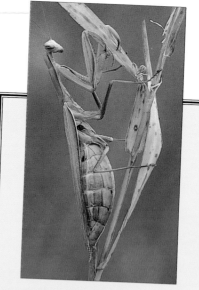

Last Wish

A male mantis needs to be very careful when mating because the female may eat his head as they do so. Even if she does decapitate him, they can still finish mating—the male has a nerve center in his lower body that allows him to continue without his head!

THERE IS NO SUCH THING AS BOY AND GIRL SNAILS; EACH SNAIL HAS BOTH MALE AND FEMALE ORGANS. THIS DOES NOT MEAN, HOWEVER, THAT THEY CAN GIVE BIRTH WITHOUT MATING; EACH SNAIL NEEDS ANOTHER TO FERTILIZE ITS EGGS.

In a World Without Predators

If all the offspring of a pair of fruit flies survived and were able to mate, and their offspring did the same, after twenty-five generations (one year) there would be enough flies to make a ball many times larger than Earth. Thank goodness for predators!

NURSERY WEB SPIDER CARRYING HER EGG SAC.

Taking Care of Baby

The goal of reproduction is to create a new, healthy generation. Eggs and young that are protected have a much better chance for survival, so adults of many species spend a lot of energy caring for them.

Female wolf spiders protect eggs and young for a brief period of time by carrying them. First they carry the eggs in an egg sac made of webbing, then, when the eggs hatch, they carry the dozen or more spiderlings on their backs.

Carrion beetles provide protection and nourishment for their young by burying a store of food. The parent beetles will bury a recently deceased mouse or other small animal and lay their eggs on it. When the larvae hatch, they can feast safely on this meal.

Growing Up

An insect changes the shape and appearance of its body as it grows. This fascinating process is called **metamorphosis,** and there are two kinds: **complete metamorphosis** and **incomplete metamorphosis.** Butterflies, moths, bees, ants, and fleas all grow through the process of complete metamorphosis. This process has four stages of growth: egg, **larva, pupa,** and adult. When the eggs hatch, wormlike young, called **larvae,** emerge. As larvae grow, they shed their skin, or **molt,** many times, because their skin, or exoskeleton, does not stretch as they grow. The larvae then stop eating and become pupae.

AS CATERPILLARS EAT, THEY GROW, AND AS THEY GROW THEY MOLT, OR SHED THEIR SKIN, MANY TIMES. TO BECOME AN ADULT, THOUGH, THEY NEED TO DO MORE THAN MOLT— THEY MUST METAMORPHOSE.

LIKE MANY INSECTS, CICADAS GROW THROUGH THE PROCESS OF INCOMPLETE METAMORPHOSIS. THIS GRAND WESTERN CICADA ADULT IS GOING THROUGH ITS LAST MOLT AS A NYMPH AND EMERGING AS AN ADULT.

WHEN THIS MONARCH CATER-PILLAR (RIGHT) GETS OLD ENOUGH, IT WILL BUILD A CHRYSALIS, OR COCOON, AROUND ITSELF. AFTER A LONG TIME INSIDE THE CHRYSALIS, IT WILL EMERGE AS A BEAUTIFUL BUTTERFLY (ABOVE).

the insects slowly change into adults. After many days, or even months, when metamorphosis is complete, adults crawl out to find a mate and start the cycle over again.

Grasshoppers, crickets, dragonflies, cockroaches, termites, and cicadas all grow through the process of incomplete metamor-phosis. This process has three stages of growth: egg, **nymph,** and adult. The nymphs that hatch out of the eggs look like small, wingless adults. As a nymph grows, it slowly changes into an adult with each molt. Its wings and repro-ductive organs slowly grow until its last molt, when it becomes an adult. The new adult is then ready to fly away and reproduce.

The vulnerable pupae are protected by their tough skin, or by cocoons, or **chrysalises,** that they make. Inside this protective shell,

Metamorphosis Miracle

To observe complete metamorphosis, you can raise mosquitoes, mealworms, or caterpillars. Mosquitoes are the easiest to observe. All you need is a bucket and some pond water.

1. Fill the bucket half full with pond water that you have filtered through a strainer to keep mosquito predators out. Add a few drops of plant food to the water to keep the algae alive (algae is the basis of the diet of young mosquitoes).

2. In warm weather, when you see adult mosquitoes flying around, place the bucket outside for a few days. With a little luck, female mosquitoes will lay their eggs in the water. The eggs of some mosquitoes float on the surface in a "raft" of eggs.

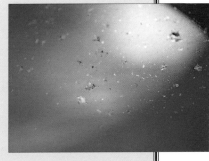

3. Keep the bucket outside or secure a mosquito-proof net on top and bring it inside. The eggs will hatch after a few days and larvae will emerge. The larvae, called **wrigglers**, will feed and swim around for a couple of weeks until they reach the pupa stage, at which time they are called **tumblers**. Adults will emerge from the tumblers after few days.

Caterpillar metamorphosis can also be easily observed. Remember, though, that this process may take close to a year because many pupae stay dormant over the winter.

1. To observe this metamorphosis, find a caterpillar and put it, along with a leafy branch from the tree you found it on, in a container. Cover this container with a lid that allows air to pass in and out.

2. Keep feeding the caterpillar fresh leaves until it creates its chrysalis, or cocoon. Weeks or months later, when the metamorphosis is complete, an adult moth or butterfly will emerge from the chrysalis.

SURVIVAL

An amazing variety of escape plans and natural defenses are present in the world of invertebrates. These range from simple, such as being colored green to blend in with surrounding plants, to complex, such as being poisonous.

Blending In

Many invertebrates are **camouflaged,** which means that they are colored and shaped like plant leaves, sticks, rocks, or even mud. Careful inspection of plants may reveal many camouflaged invertebrates.

FOR A SPECIES TO SURVIVE, THE ADULTS MUST LIVE LONG ENOUGH TO REPRODUCE AND LAY EGGS. THIS QUESTION MARK BUTTERFLY HAS CAMOUFLAGE COLORING THAT HELPS IT TO HIDE FROM PREDATORS.

Can't Catch Me

Many animals rely on speed to escape predators or other dangers. Cockroaches can hear the footsteps of an approaching person, and are able to run away at speeds of up to a foot (0.3 meters) per second. Because of this, they are rarely seen by people.

Walking sticks feed on oak, locust, cherry, and walnut leaves. They escape predators by having bodies and legs that look like branches swaying in the wind. Being mud-colored may not seem glamorous, but for snails, worms, and insects that live in muddy water, it is the ideal defense. With this camouflage, these invertebrates are able to move around in the water and remain unseen by predators. Phantom midge larvae, though, live in clear water, and would therefore be easily seen by predators if they were mud-colored. For this reason, they are almost clear, and predators are unable to see them. These larvae have the perfect non-disguise. Some invertebrates do not have natural camouflage, and must therefore create their own. Spider crabs and hermit crabs attach small plants and

Hair Coloring

Head lice are parasites of people. Many head lice can camouflage themselves as they grow by becoming the same color as the person's hair. They feed by biting the skin and sucking small drops of blood.

ABOVE: TRILOBITE BEETLES LOOK LIKE MASSES OF LEAVES AND FERNS THAT HAVE FALLEN TO THE GROUND. ABOVE RIGHT: ANOTHER COMMON DEFENSE IS WARNING: THE SMALL EASTERN MILKWEED BUG IS BRIGHTLY COLORED TO WARN PREDATORS THAT IT IS POISONOUS TO EAT.

animals to their shells to make themselves appear to be a part of the ocean floor. Caddisfly larvae create their own camouflage by cementing together bits and pieces of sand and plants into a tube. They live in this tube, carrying it around as if it were a tiny mobile home. Because each species of caddisfly uses different kinds of material for its home, entomologists can determine each fly's species by studying the materials used for its home.

THESE LEAFHOPPERS USE ONE OF THE MOST COMMON INVERTEBRATE DEFENSES: CAMOUFLAGE. THEY LOOK LIKE LEAVES OR BUDS OF THE PLANTS THEY INHABIT.

Keep Away

Not all invertebrates are camouflaged. Some, in fact, are brightly colored to stand out from their surroundings. This is because they have very strong defenses and want predators to know.

The bright orange X on milkweed bugs and the bright colors of monarch butterflies advertise that they are poisonous. Milkweed bugs and monarch butterflies, unlike most animals, are able to digest the poisons found in milkweed plants. These poisons accumulate in their bodies and make them unpleasant eating for most predators.

The bright colors of ladybugs announce their ability to secrete yellow liquids that smell and taste very bad. Most predators are

Camouflage Trail

For a fun game that tests the observation skills of the players and gives you some ideas about what colors or shapes serve as good camouflage, create a Camouflage Trail for your friends and family.

1. The trail can be located in the woods, in a nearby field, or even in a room of your house or school. Create the trail by selecting about ten objects of different shapes and colors.

2. You can make objects that look like insects or other invertebrates, or you can use colored paper in different shapes, pipe cleaners, rubber bands, or toilet paper tubes.

3. Place these objects in the area you selected for the trail, but make sure they are all visible (do not hide any behind a tree).

4. Have your friends walk slowly down the trail one at a time and count how many hidden objects they find. Tell them not to pick up any of the objects.

5. After everyone has looked, show them where all the objects are. Which objects were camouflaged the best? Which was more important for a good disguise: color or shape?

SOME INVERTEBRATES ESCAPE BEING EATEN BY PREDATORS BECAUSE THEIR COLORING RESEMBLES THAT OF POISONOUS INVERTEBRATES. THE VICEROY BUTTERFLY (BOTTOM) MIMICS THE COLORATION AND PATTERN OF THE FOUL-TASTING MONARCH (ABOVE).

unable or unwilling to eat a ladybug that has secreted these smelly liquids.

Look-alikes

Some invertebrates only look like they have strong defenses. The coloration of these animals closely resembles, or **mimics**, poisonous or dangerous animals. These mimics are therefore able to avoid predators, even though they do not have strong defenses. For example, viceroy butterflies, which are not poisonous, would make a good meal for any predator. But because their coloration mimics the color patterns of

monarch butterflies, which are poisonous, most predators ignore them.

An insect's coloration, though, does not need to mimic a whole animal to be effective. Many butterflies and moths have "eye spots" on their wings. The eye spots trick predators into thinking that the insect is actually a much larger animal.

Smelly Headstand

When darkling beetles are threatened, they do headstands and spray foul-smelling liquids from glands located at the end of their abdomen. When a grasshopper mouse catches one of these beetles, it immediately sticks the beetle's abdomen into the ground to avoid the spray. Then it eats the beetle head first.

Hot Shot

In Africa and Asia there are many different kinds of bombardier beetles. Some of these beetles can shoot smelly liquids that are as hot as 212°F (100°C). When attacked, these insects spray chemicals from their abdomens. The chemicals mix in the air and create a small explosion.

Turnabout

The art of camouflage is not limited to those being hunted. Many predators are also camouflaged to match their surroundings. Some mantises are colored leaf-green and are difficult even for people to see. The praying mantis got its name because of the way it "hunts" —as it waits for a victim it appears to be praying. When an insect walks by, though, the mantis immediately springs into action.

Some species of crab spider also have special camouflage abilities. They are able to change their color to match the yellow and white flowers they hide on.

JUST AS SOME INVERTEBRATES USE CAMOUFLAGE TO PREVENT THEIR BEING EATEN, SOME PREDATORS USE CAMOUFLAGE TO CATCH THEIR PREY. THE CRAB SPIDER HUNTS BY DISGUISING ITSELF AS PART OF A FLOWER'S HEAD.

Deadly Attractions

Bolas spiders (above) give off odors that resemble the pheromones of female moths. Male moths are attracted to this smell and fly toward the spider. The spider catches moths by swinging strands of silk at them. The moths get stuck on a drop of sticky fluid at the end of the silk and are reeled in.

A predator called a **photuris** mimics the flashes of some female fireflies. This attracts male fireflies to the hungry photuris.

THE GREEN LEAF MIMIC PRAYING MANTIS FOOLS ITS PREY BY HIDING AMONG A GROUP OF LEAVES.

CHAPTER FOUR

LIVING TOGETHER

THIS TUSSOCK MOTH CATERPILLAR WILL QUICKLY DEVOUR THIS LEAF AND MOVE ON TO ANOTHER. IF A TREE IS INFESTED BY MANY CATERPILLARS, IT CAN LOSE MOST OF ITS LEAVES TO THESE RAVENOUS CREATURES.

Housing an Army

The bull's horn acacia (a plant that is native to Central America) has large hollow thorns that ants use as shelters. Ant colonies that set up home in these thorns will defend the plant against any danger. People who have bumped into one of these plants have regretted it because many of the ants can give painful bites.

PARASITISM AND MUTUALISM

When it comes to finding food and shelter, many invertebrates get their food in one place and their shelter in another. Some find both food and shelter in one place, such as on a plant or an animal. Sometimes this relationship is harmful to the plant or animal, called a **host**, and sometimes it is helpful. When an invertebrate harms its host in this search for food and shelter, the relationship is referred to as **parasitism** (and the invertebrate is called a **parasite**). When the relationship helps the host, it is referred to as **mutualism**.

Plant Hosts

Many invertebrates, both parasitic and mutualistic, have plants as hosts. Mourning cloak caterpillars, for instance, feed on leaves and are parasites of poplar, elm, hackberry, and willow trees. These caterpillars have such large appetites that they can strip a small tree of its leaves.

Many wasps are parasites of oak trees and goldenrod plants. Female wasps lay their eggs in the plants' tissues. When the wasp larvae hatch out of the eggs, they give off a chemical that causes the plant to grow a protective **gall** (a swelling of the plant tissue) around the larvae. The larvae grow in these living nurseries

Gall Investigation

Galls are large round growths that can be found on many plants. They are caused by fungi, mites, and many insects. Galls can be examined outside on the plants or brought inside for observation and dissection. Look on oak tree branches or on goldenrod plants for galls, and examine the galls for any tiny holes. A hole indicates that the insect inside has already left.

If you would like to bring the gall inside, cut the branch at an angle and insert the cut end of the branch in a glass of water to keep the branch and the insect larva alive. Place the gall in an aquarium or other container that has a secure lid but allows air to pass in. Check every day to see if the adult insect has emerged.

You might also choose to dissect the gall before the adult insect emerges. To do so, carefully cut open the gall, with the help of an adult, and look for the young larva inside.

until they are old enough to tunnel out.

Not all invertebrates, however, harm the plants they get their food from. The relationship between many flowering plants and flying insects is mutualistic. The sweet nectar that many of these plants produce serves as food for the insects, and the insects in turn help the plants to reproduce by carrying pollen from plant to plant.

ABOVE: SOME WASPS, FRUIT FLIES, AND OTHER INSECTS GROW UP INSIDE GALLS. THE HOLES IN THIS BLUEBERRY PEPPER BOX GALL SHOW THAT THE YOUNG MATURED AND ATE THEIR WAY OUT. RIGHT: THE RELATIONSHIP BETWEEN BEES AND FLOWERS IS ONE OF THE BEST-KNOWN EXAMPLES OF MUTUALISM.

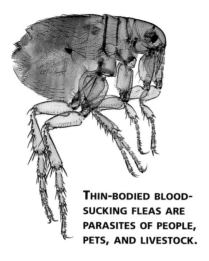

THIN-BODIED BLOOD-SUCKING FLEAS ARE PARASITES OF PEOPLE, PETS, AND LIVESTOCK.

Animal Hosts

Animals can be hosts to hundreds of parasitic invertebrates. These parasites may eat dead skin, live skin, body secretions, or even blood. Mosquitoes, fleas, lice, leeches, and other blood-sucking parasites harm their hosts not only by taking nutrient-rich blood,

but frequently by passing on diseases as well. Hundreds of years ago, for instance, rat fleas helped spread the Bubonic Plague (also known as the Black Death), which killed millions of people in Europe.

Female mosquitoes drink the blood of many different kinds of animals, including humans. When a mosquito

Not all parasites suck blood, however. Some, like ichneumon wasps, are considered parasites because they feed live insects to their young. Ichneumon wasps are parasites of caterpillars, beetles, flies, and many other crop pests. Cicadas, which are pests of plant roots, are parasitized by cicada killer ichneumon

THIS WASP WILL USE THE CICADA IT HAS CAUGHT AND PARALYZED AS A LIVING MEAL FOR ITS SOON-TO-HATCH LARVAE.

Getting Their Fill

Blood is a very nutritious meal, but it is not always easy to find. In an effort to make the most of each meal, leeches, like female mosquitoes, swell to accommodate as much blood as possible. Unlike mosquitoes, however, leeches are able to make each meal last a long time. One meal of nutrient-rich blood can sustain a leech for at least a month, sometimes even up to a year.

finds a host, it lands and inserts its needlelike mouth, called a **beak**, into the animal's skin. Its abdomen swells as it drinks up to its own body weight in blood! Mosquitoes inject chemicals into the host to help the blood flow. These chemicals give the bite the itchy feeling we are all familiar with. The nutritious blood allows the female mosquitoes to produce large numbers of healthy eggs.

wasps. The cicadas are caught and paralyzed with a sting by adult female cicada killers. The paralyzed cicadas are then taken to the wasp's burrow, packed tightly into it, and eaten alive by the wasp's larvae.

Invertebrates find food and shelter on all kinds of plants and animals, including people. In fact, there are very few, if any, plants or animals that are not host to some invertebrates.

SOCIAL INSECTS

Ants, honeybees, and termites are all social insects that thrive in many areas of the world. Social insects are insects that live in large groups, or **colonies**. (A large ant nest, for instance, may house close to 300,000 ants!) Social insects construct nests, hives, and burrows to house the many members of the colony, and they work together to find food and protect their large, intricate homes.

Termite Champions

Termites are **herbivores** (that is, they eat only plants) that live in large nests. The largest recorded termite nest, which was found in Australia, was close to 18 feet (5.5 meters) high and 90 feet (27.4 meters) across. One of these nests can contain five million termites. Termite queens can lay up to one egg every three seconds and live for up to fifty years.

Taking Care of Ants

If you would like to keep ants as pets, you can buy an ant farm from the store or create your own in an aquarium or other glass container. The container will need to have a secure, antproof top that will also allow air to pass through. Tape black paper onto the outside of one side of the glass container—ants like to tunnel in dark areas. (To observe the tunnels, take off the paper periodically.) Fill the container with moist, loose soil (preferably taken from where the ants live).

Before you collect your ants, make sure that you are familiar with any harmful ant species, such as fire ants, living in your area. Once you have the ants, place them in the container with some fresh leaves and pieces of fruit. After a week or two, return the ants to the place where you found them.

Active Ants

Due to their sheer numbers and their roles as both predators and prey, ants are important members of many habitats. All ants are social, and most are predators of caterpillars and other small animals. Their nests are usually underground, but some species construct their nests in dead trees or even in the wood of people's homes.

Ant colonies start off small and eventually grow to have thousands of members. Sometimes a few male ants are raised—the colony needs males to mate with new queens—but most of the members are female workers. These workers are

THE EATING HABITS OF ANTS DIFFER FROM SPECIES TO SPECIES, BUT ALL SPECIES ARE SOCIAL ANIMALS— THEY LIVE AND WORK TOGETHER TO ACCOMPLISH THE GOALS OF THE GROUP. TOP: THESE LEAF-CUTTER ANTS WORK TOGETHER TO GATHER ENOUGH PLANT MATERIAL TO KEEP THEIR UNDERGROUND GARDENS OF FUNGUS ALIVE. ABOVE: SOME SPECIES OF ANTS ARE SCAVENGERS. THEY TAKE DEAD ANIMALS, LIKE THIS GRASSHOPPER, BACK TO THEIR COLONY TO BE EATEN.

sterile, meaning they cannot lay eggs. It is their job to collect food, defend the colony, repair the nest, and tend to the queen and her eggs. Ants are very strong for their size. If you were proportionately as strong as an ant, you would be able to lift many tons!

Every year, young queens leave the nest to mate and start new hives. After mating, a queen finds a good location, rips off her wings (she does not need to fly any more), builds a small nest, and lays her first eggs. She will never have to mate again, because she stores the male's sperm in her body. Soon after her first few workers are born, she devotes all her time to laying eggs. The workers, meanwhile, begin enlarging the nest and protecting their new colony.

Ants are able to communicate with each other by using chemicals called **pheromones**. Workers use pheromones to make "scent trails" as they forage for food. They use these to find their way back to the nest and to lead other workers to the food they found. Ants use many different

Fungus Farmers

The leaf-cutter ants of Central America collect pieces of leaves, but they do not eat them. The leaves are fed to **fungi** (organisms similar to mushrooms that live on rotting matter) in the ants' nest. The ants then harvest and eat the fungus. This fungus is dependent on the ants and would quickly die without the ants' careful farming.

kinds of pheromones, each of which has its own special message. Some pheromones are used to show the way to food, while others are used to indicate danger. Still others are used to attract mates.

IN A COLONY, EACH MEMBER OF THE GROUP HAS A SPECIFIC JOB. SOME OF THESE COCKTAIL ANTS (ABOVE) WILL DEVOTE THEIR LIVES TO THE CARE OF THE QUEEN'S LARVAE. THIS CARPENTER ANT QUEEN (RIGHT), LIKE THE QUEEN OF ANY ANT OR TERMITE COLONY, IS PAMPERED AND CAREFULLY PROTECTED.

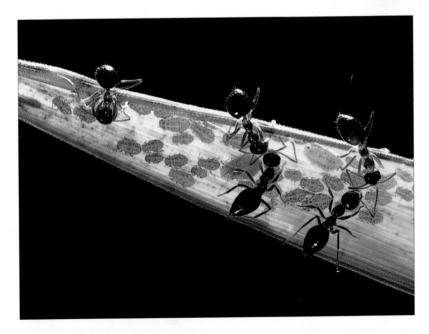

SOME INVERTEBRATES ARE FARMERS! THESE CORNFIELD ANTS TEND TO AND PROTECT APHIDS. THIS IS A MUTUALLY BENEFICIAL RELATIONSHIP: THE APHIDS BENEFIT BY BEING PROTECTED BY THE LARGER, STRONGER INSECTS; THE ANTS BENEFIT BY EATING THE APHIDS' SWEET WASTES.

Tiny Farmers

Over much of North America, cornfield ants take care of aphids. In this mutualistic relationship, the cornfield ants are said to "farm" the aphids. Adult aphids lay their eggs in the ants' nests and the ants tend them. When the young aphids hatch, they are carried by the ants to the roots of corn plants. As the aphids suck the juices of the plants, they secrete their waste, a sweet fluid that the ants in turn use for food.

HONEYBEES COLLECT NECTAR FROM FLOWERS TO MAKE HONEY.

Sweet Insects

A 9,000-year-old cave painting in Spain shows a person robbing a wild honeybee hive of its honey. Today, beeswax and honey are still widely used all over the world. There are many species of bees in North America, but honeybees are not native to the continent (that is, they originally came from another part of the world). They were introduced to North America a few hundred years ago by European settlers.

The inside of a honeybee hive is very busy. Up to sixty thousand sterile female workers tend to one queen and a few hundred male drones. There is an order, or **succession,** of duties that sterile female workers undertake during their

brief six- to eight-week lives. As they age, their jobs change in the following order: clean the hive, feed the larvae, repair the hive, protect the hive, and collect pollen and nectar.

When a worker bee returns to the hive with pollen and nectar, it dances the "waggle dance." This

dance tells the other workers where a particular food source is located. By placing food sources in different locations and observing the "waggle dance," scientists have been able to learn how the dance works.

As honeybee workers follow the instructions of the "waggle dance" and fly from flower to flower, they store nectar in their **crop** (a stomachlike organ). Upon returning to the hive, they **regurgitate,** or vomit up, the nectar and mix it with air and special chemicals in their saliva. They then chew it until it becomes honey. Any honey

INSIDE A BEEHIVE WORKER BEES BUILD MANY HONEYCOMBS. THESE SMALL "ROOMS" ARE USED TO STORE HONEY AND AS LIVING SPACES FOR HONEYBEE YOUNG.

Protecting the Hive

Honeybee workers will defend their queen and the hive with their lives. Deep inside the hive, the queen is constantly attended as she lays up to a thousand eggs a day. Outside the hive, workers are ready to attack any animal that threatens the colony. Each honeybee has a stinger in its abdomen that it thrusts out in an attack. Unfortunately for the bee, though, this means its own death—when a bee stings, it damages its abdomen and dies shortly after.

WHEN A HIVE GETS TOO FULL, BEES WILL SWARM, AS THEY ARE DOING HERE. THE OLD QUEEN AND A LARGE PORTION OF THE COLONY WILL FLY OFF IN SEARCH OF A NEW HOME.

that is not immediately eaten is stored in honeycombs for later use.

The colonies that these social insects live in have often been compared to human societies. Both populations live in large groups and have very specific rules about behavior, but the lifestyles of the two are very different, to say the least. Social insects, though, are fascinating invertebrates and are worthy of close examination.

Langstroth Hive

A modern commercial honeybee hive is called a Langstroth hive. This hive, which has separate removable sections in which worker bees raise young or store honey, was designed in the United States in 1851. Beekeepers wear protective clothing and calm the bees down with smoke before taking honey from the hive. The queen and young live in a section called the **brood chamber** and the honey is stored in the **super.** The super is taken apart to collect the honey, but some is always left for the bees to eat.

THE MOVE IS ON

Long and short journeys are common among invertebrates. Many travel short distances to find new homes or food, while others travel hundreds, sometimes thousands, of miles to escape cold winter weather. Overcrowding can also force them to make long journeys. Many invertebrates cannot fly and are unable to escape these diffi-culties, but butterflies, dragonflies, bees, and locusts have been able to survive by using their wings.

Magnificent Migrations

During late summer and into the fall, butterflies and dragonflies travel, or **migrate**, great distances. Monarch butterflies that live in Canada and the northern United States fly south to warmer climates in the southern United States. It was recently discovered that they even fly as far south as the mountains of central Mexico. They travel during the day, fluttering their way south, and rest at night, completely covering trees and other plants as they huddle in large groups. Question mark, painted lady, and red admi-ral butterflies also migrate south, but they fly only as

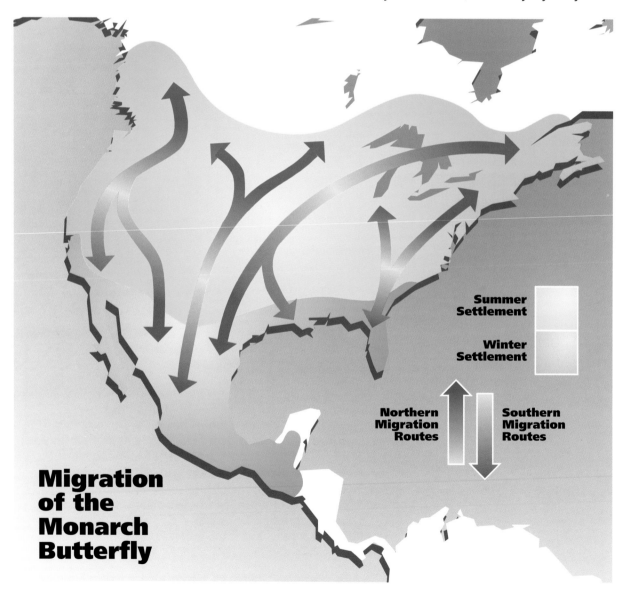

Summer Settlement

Winter Settlement

Northern Migration Routes

Southern Migration Routes

Migration of the Monarch Butterfly

THE MONARCHS THAT SUCCESSFULLY MIGRATE SOUTH TO THE MOUNTAINS OF CENTRAL MEXICO GATHER ON TREES IN LARGE MASSES TO REST.

far as the Carolinas and northern Florida.

Many species of dragonflies also migrate south in the fall, but their destination is unknown. In the northeastern United States during late summer, swarms of dragonflies, such as green darners, black mantled gliders, and globetrotters, can be seen traveling south along the coast. As they migrate, they eat mosraised in preparation for quitoes, flies, and other pests. The dragonflies in turn become food for many fly-catching birds, including phoebes and kingbirds.

Insect Clouds

When a beehive becomes overcrowded, the bees swarm (that is, the queen leaves with a large group of the workers to form a new hive). Young queens are the swarm, but it is the old queen that leaves. The young queens stay and battle it out to see who will rule over the bees. Usually the firstborn is able to kill the others before they reach adulthood. When a good location is found, the new hive is built. In northern climates, it is important that the new hive is stocked with lots of honey before winter sets in. The workers must collect a lot of nectar before it gets too cold or the hive will die during the winter.

Locusts (a kind of grasshopper) also swarm, but their reason for doing so is to search for food. As they swarm, they often devastate the land as they devour its vegetation. A single swarm may cover up to two thousand square miles (5,180 square kilometers), and may be made up of billions of locusts. Locust swarms have even been seen 1,200 miles (1,932 kilometers) off the coast. Locusts swarm in many parts of the world, including the western United States. The impact of the swarming locusts is not entirely destructive, though. They also serve as important sources of food for many birds and other animals.

CHAPTER FIVE

SEARCHING THE HABITATS

INVERTEBRATES CAN BE FOUND IN MANY DIFFERENT HABITATS. EVEN A SMALL PATCH OF NATURE, SUCH AS A BACKYARD, GARDEN, OR VACANT LOT, CAN BE HOME TO A MYRIAD OF INVERTEBRATES.

SEARCHING THE HABITATS

Nature has a lot to offer those who are curious enough to explore its habitats, which are home to many beautiful and fascinating plants and animals. While it is true that there are thousands of invertebrates to observe, there are also trees, wildflowers, and small vertebrate animals that are also fun and exciting to investigate. And some of these habitats are no farther away than your backyard.

Many invertebrates are most active at night. Animals that feed and mate at night and rest during the day are called **nocturnal** animals. As night approaches, invertebrates begin their mating calls. It is at this time that we hear their pleasant sounds and see their beautiful flashing lights. Moths, beetles, and other nocturnal flying insects are attracted to bright lights. On a dark night, you can see dozens of different beetles, flies, and moths flying around the lights outside your house.

Bright Light Attraction

The attraction of nocturnal flying insects to bright lights is called **phototaxis**. The insects are attracted to the lights because the light affects their flight paths. If an insect is near a light source, the wings on one side of its body beat slower than the wings on the other side, causing the insect to turn toward the light. As a result, it spirals helplessly into the bright light.

Household

You need not search far to observe invertebrates. Many of them live in our homes with us. Flies, crickets, moths, spiders, and cockroaches find food and shelter in our walls, beds, and kitchen pantries—and even on our bodies. German cockroaches, which are abundant in many city environments, eat almost anything, including leftover pet and people food, and even the glue found in wallpaper, on stamps, and in the bindings of books.

Backyard and Garden

Backyard and garden habitats provide food and shelter for ground-dwelling earthworms, centipedes, and beetle larvae. They are also home to plant-dwelling butterflies and bees and predatory invertebrates such as spiders.

People spend a great deal of time and money to rid lawns and gardens of invertebrate pests, but it is often difficult to tell which are pests and which are not. Ants and earthworms are helpful to many plants, but cicadas and many beetles are harmful to many plants.

TOP: **VISITORS FROM OUTSIDE, LIKE THIS DADDY LONGLEGS, MAY OCCASIONALLY WANDER INTO OUR HOMES. MIDDLE: CENTIPEDES MAY BE FOUND LIVING IN AND AROUND YOUR BACKYARD. IF YOU UNCOVER ONE, IT WILL SCURRY AWAY TO FIND A NEW PLACE TO HIDE. BOTTOM: GARDENS ARE GREAT PLACES TO FIND ALL KINDS OF INVERTEBRATES, LIKE THIS BUFFALO TREEHOPPER.**

Jar of Invertebrates

To catch crawling invertebrates, dig a hole in the ground and bury a glass jar in the soil up to its rim.

Then place something over the jar, such as a raised wooden board, that provides shade but also allows the invertebrates to crawl under. Check the jar every few hours, and observe the creatures you have caught. Be careful with your invertebrate pets, and be sure to release them when you are finished observing them.

LEFT: FIELDS, WITH THEIR FLOWERS AND GRASSES, ATTRACT MANY KINDS OF INVERTEBRATES, FROM NECTAR-GATHERING, FLYING INSECTS TO WEB-WEAVING, PREDATORY SPIDERS. INSET: THIS AMERICAN PAINTED LADY BUTTERFLY IS JUST ONE OF THE MANY BEAUTIFULLY COLORED INSECTS YOU MAY SEE IN A FIELD.

Field and Forest

Wildflowers and tall field grasses attract flying, crawling, and hopping invertebrates. Butterflies and honeybees search for nectar, grasshoppers and beetles look for succulent plants, and praying mantises and spiders hunt most of the other invertebrates.

Woodlands, with their great diversity of habitats, contain hundreds of different species of invertebrates. Springtails, earwigs, slugs, centipedes, millipedes, and pill woodlouses find nourishment and shelter underneath rotten logs. Termites, ants, and many kinds of insect larvae chew the

Weather Report

For an interesting experiment on the effects of weather on invertebrate life, measure the daily temperature changes that occur in different habitats near you.

1. Make a chart so that you can record the information you gather. You will need a sturdy thermometer that you can hang outside, bury in the soil, or float in a pond. Possible sites include the outside of your house, the soil of your garden or lawn, and the water in a nearby pond or lake.

2. Measure the temperature for each area you select every day or every other day. Measure soil temperature by digging a small hole and inserting the thermometer into the soil for a few minutes. Ask an adult to help you measure the temperature in a pond or lake by tying a string to the thermometer and gently tossing the thermometer into the water a few feet from the shore. Be careful not to throw it into an area where it will get stuck.

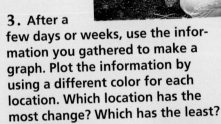

3. After a few days or weeks, use the information you gathered to make a graph. Plot the information by using a different color for each location. Which location has the most change? Which has the least?

LEFT: PONDS AND OTHER WET-LANDS ARE TREASURE TROVES OF INVERTEBRATES. IN SOME LOCA-TIONS, YOU CAN FIND AQUATIC, TERRESTRIAL, AND FLYING INVERTE-BRATES BY THE HUNDREDS. INSET: WATER STRIDERS ARE AMONG THE PREDATORY INVERTEBRATES YOU MAY SEE WHEN YOU VISIT A POND.

Nocturnal Gathering

To prove that phototaxis really exists, you can attract nocturnal flying insects with a bright light and a white sheet.

1. Go outside on a warm, dark night and bring a bright light with you.

2. Put the white cloth in the way of the beam of light by stretching it between two tree branches.

After a few minutes, you should be able to see many beetles, moths, and flies resting on the sheet. How many different kinds did you attract? To see different insects, try this activity at different times during the spring and summer.

decaying wood inside rotten logs into pulp. And wasps, beetles, and caterpillars make nurseries and eat the leaves, fruit, and seeds of live trees.

Ponds

The still waters of ponds are filled with fascinating invertebrates. Snails and many worms feed on pieces of dead animals and plants found in mud and leaf litter. Striders and water measurers patrol the water's surface for struggling insects that may have fallen from overhanging plants. Predatory giant water bugs, lesser boatmen, saucer bugs, and backswimmers can be found swimming in ponds. These insects breathe air but can survive underwater for short periods of time by carrying bubbles of air with them as they dive in search of food. Mosquitoes and dragonflies are among the many pond-dwelling invertebrates that spend only part of their lives in water. When these insects metamorphose into adults, they crawl out of the water and fly away.

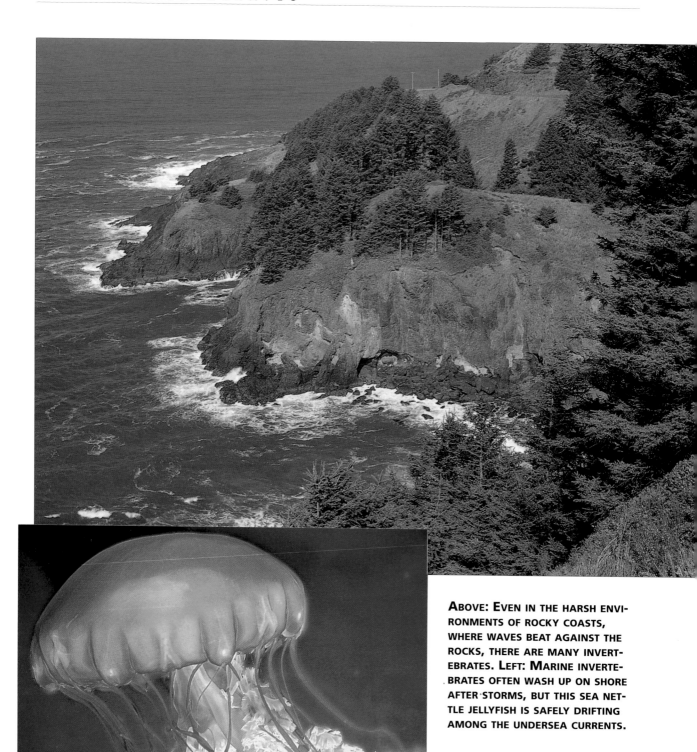

**ABOVE: EVEN IN THE HARSH ENVI-
RONMENTS OF ROCKY COASTS,
WHERE WAVES BEAT AGAINST THE
ROCKS, THERE ARE MANY INVERT-
EBRATES. LEFT: MARINE INVERTE-
BRATES OFTEN WASH UP ON SHORE
AFTER STORMS, BUT THIS SEA NET-
TLE JELLYFISH IS SAFELY DRIFTING
AMONG THE UNDERSEA CURRENTS.**

The Shore

There are also many fascinating invertebrates to be found on the sand and rocks of beaches and in the waves of the ocean. Clam worms, moon snails, and sand dollars crawl through the sand in search of food, while mussels and periwinkle snails cling to rocks as waves crash around them.

The remains of ocean-dwelling animals, such as crabs, snails, jellyfish, sea urchins, and sea stars, can be found among the debris on many beaches. This debris was washed up onshore by waves or dropped onto the beach by gulls or other predators. During low tide, sea urchins, sea stars, crabs, snails, and young lobsters can be found on rocky beaches waiting in tidal pools for the high tide to arrive and set them free.

Name Games

Horseshoe crabs are not really crabs, but distant relatives of spiders! They live in the ocean along the eastern coast of the United States and spend their time burrowing through the sand and mud in search of worms and other small invertebrates to eat. Each spring, they crawl into shallow water to mate and lay greenish eggs.

HERMIT CRABS ARE CRABS THAT LIVE IN SNAIL SHELLS. THIS SHELL USED TO BELONG TO A **WHELK** (A KIND OF SNAIL), BUT AFTER THE WHELK DIED THE HERMIT CRAB CLAIMED ITS SHELL.

BIBLIOGRAPHY

Children's Books

Althea. *Insects and Other Small Creatures*. Memphis, Tenn.: Troll Associates, 1990.

Braus, Judy, ed. *Incredible Insects*. Washington, D.C.: National Wildlife Federation, 1984.

Leahy, Christopher. *Peterson First Guides: Insects*. Boston: Houghton Miffin Co., 1987.

Mound, Laurence. *Insect.* New York: Alfred A. Knopf, 1990.

Owen, Jennifer. *Insect Life*. London: Usborne Publishing Ltd., 1984.

Parker, Steve. *Insects.* New York: Dorling Kindersley, 1992.

Pringle, Laurence. *The Golden Book of Insects and Spiders*. Racine, Wis.: Western Publishing Co., 1990.

Zim, Herbert S. *Insects.* Racine, Wis.: Golden Press, 1987.

Young Adult Books

Doris, Ellen. *Entomology*. New York: Thames and Hudson, 1993.

_____. *Invertebrate Zoology*. New York: Thames and Hudson, 1993.

Bush, Pauline. *Insect World*. Alexandria, Va.: Time-Life Books, 1988.

Mitchell, Robert. *Butterflies and Moths*. Racine, Wis.: Golden Press, 1962.

Reid, George. *Pond Life*. Racine, Wis.: Golden Press, 1967.

Reference/Guidebooks

Begon, Michael. *Ecology.* Sunderland, Mass.: Sinauer Assoc., Inc., 1986.

Curtis, Helen. *Biology.* New York: Worth Publishers, Inc., 1983.

Fitcher, George. *Insect Pests*. Racine, Wis.: Golden Press, 1966.

Gosner, Kenneth. *Peterson Field Guides: Atlantic Seashore*. Boston: Houghton Miffin Co., 1978.

Kricher, John C. *Peterson Field Guides: Eastern Forests*. Boston: Houghton Miffin Co., 1988.

Levi, Herbert. *A Guide to Spiders*. Racine, Wis.: Golden Press, 1968.

Morris, Percy A. *Peterson Field Guides: Shells of the Atalantic*. Boston: Houghton Mifflin Co., 1975.

Pechenik, Jan. *Biology of the Invertebrates*. Boston: Prindle, Weber & Schnidt, 1985.

Villee, Claude. *General Zoology*. Philadelphia: Saunders College Publishing, 1984.

Wernert, Susan, ed. *North American Wildlife*. Pleasantville, N.Y.: Readers Digest, 1982.

Specimen and Supply Companies

Carolina Biological Supply
2700 York Road
Burlington, NC 27215

Carolina Biological Supply
Box 187
Gladstone, OR 97027

Science Kit, Inc.
777 East Park Drive
Tonawanda, NY 14150

Wards Natural Science
P.O. Box 92912
Rochester, NY 14692

INDEX

*Numbers in italics
indicate illustrations.*

PHOTO CREDITS